Kalia and Joey's Treasures

By Linda Sue Svoboda

PUBLISHED *by* PARABLES
Earthly Stories with a Heavenly Meaning

Kalia and Joey's Treasures

By

Linda Sue Svoboda

PUBLISHED by PARABLES

Earthly Stories with a Heavenly Meaning

Kalia and Joey's Treasures

By

Linda Sue Svoboda

PUBLISHED *by* PARABLES
Earthly Stories with a Heavenly Meaning

Dedication

This book is lovingly dedicated to my precious family. We have been blessed with some amazing pets over the years. For that, I am so incredibly thankful.

Kalia and Joey's Treasures

Kalia had always loved cats. She loved big, beautiful cats, and sweet little kittens as well. Her dream had always been to have her own kitten someday. Every time  she saw a tiny kitten, or a bigger cat, she would beg her Mom and Dad to have one of her very own.

"I am sure that it will happen someday, sweet-heart. Just keep dreaming, hoping, and praying.   I am sure that it will happen when the perfect time is right," her Mom said.

A few weeks later, her Dad got a very important phone call. His relatives, who lived on a farm, shared some wonderful news. A new litter of kittens had been  born, and they wondered if everyone would like to see them in about 8 weeks. After hanging up the phone, Dad called a family meeting for Mom, Kalia, and her big brother, Joey. Everyone was so excited to see what Dad was going to say, especially because this was the Christmas season.

"Everyone, please come and sit down. I have some exciting news to share. I know that everyone loves cats, and I know how wonderful it would be to have  a cat of our own. And, Kalia, I know that you have been hoping and dreaming of owning a pet for a long time. Our relatives on the farm called, and wanted to let us know that their Mama cat had a litter of 8 kittens that were born last week. If we wanted to pick one out, they said that they would love that!"

With that amazing news, both Kalia and Joey started jumping up and down. They held hands, and danced around the living room.

"Yes! I know both of us would love that, Dad." Joey said happily.

Kalia ran to her Mom, and gave her the biggest hug ever. With tears in her  eyes, her Mom glanced happily at her husband. For, she had always loved cats too. This would be a dream of hers coming true as well.

The next 8 weeks went by slowly for Kalia and Joey, but their Mom and Dad filled the days with a lot of special activities and plans for their adoption of a new kitten. They bought litter,

kitten food, new toys, and they prepared a part in the house reserved just for the new kitten to sleep.

Soon, it was time to make the trek to see the new kitten. Everyone was excited as they all piled into their minivan. The time went so quickly. When they arrived at the home of their  relatives, the kids couldn't wait to see the kittens. Their cousins led them to the place where all of the kittens were sleeping and playing. Even though there were 8 kittens, Joey and Kalia immediately went to a little black and white kitten, who was playing by himself. He soon ran under a tree. He was so cute, and had beautiful black and white markings all over his side and his tail.

"Oh, Mom, he is so beautiful, and so very little. I just love him!" With that, Kalia picked him up, and gave him a big hug. "You need to hold him too, Joey."

Joey held him for a long time. "I would like to name him Oreo."

He saw his Mom and Dad talking with a smile on their faces. In a happy voice, he heard his Dad say, "Kids, I think you made a wonderful choice in choosing that sweet kitten. Naming him Oreo sounds awesome, Joey. But Mom and I think that we should adopt one more. That way, they won't get lonely, and they will be best friends."

"Really Dad? Boy, that is the best news ever!" Joey stated happily.

Mom and Dad took turns holding a little Calico. She had wide eyes, and started purring immediately. "I like this one, honey. There is something about her that is so spunky. I think that she and her brother would get along very well at our home," their Mom said with a smile on her face. "What would you like to name her, Kalia?"

"She looks like a Brea to me," Kalia said happily. "Then, I can call her Bree for short."

"Oh, they are just the cutest

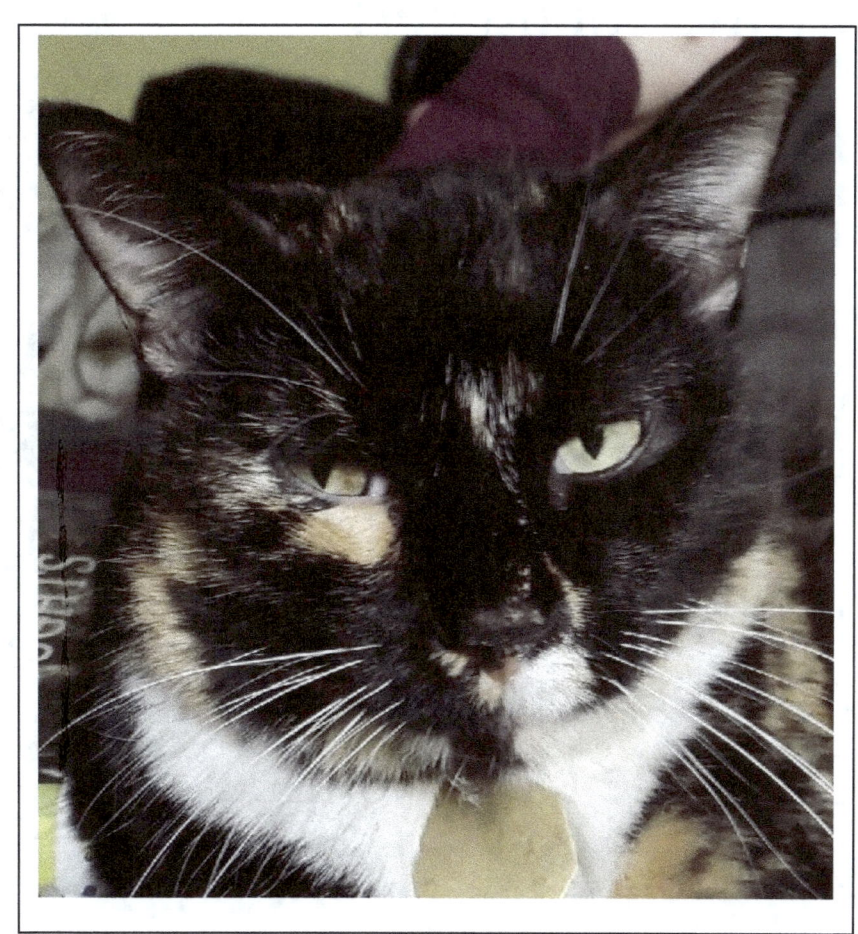

kittens ever!" With huge grins on their faces, the kids knew that this happy day would stay in their memory banks forever.

Over the years, Oreo and Bree made quite an impression on the young family. Oreo played hide and seek with Kalia in the basement. He was so smart, that he always found her!

Oreo had the same markings and personality of their Mother's childhood cat, Cutie Pie. Every time she saw Oreo, wonderful memories of Cutie Pie came to the surface.

Oreo and Bree loved cuddling up together. They enjoyed snuggling with each other, and it looked like they were hugging each other with all of their

hearts. They also loved the windows, and had fun watching the birds and the squirrels. They were so very happy.

Oreo loved to sit and be with Dad when he worked in his home office. Oreo loved to "knead" Dad's stomach, and Dad always got a kick out of

that. He also knew exactly when Joey would come home from school, and he would wait by the door. Joey would then take him outside, and let him play in the grass. And often the snow!

As the kids grew up, so did Oreo and Bree. Soon Joey brought a wonderful new girlfriend home to meet everyone. Adrianna saw everyone with Dad holding

Oreo, and Kalia holding Bree. They said, "Welcome to our home. We love our fur babies so much!" Soon, Oreo went to

Jonathan, and he held him so gently and

kindly. Adrianna saw that, and she said, "Wow, that is so awesome to meet you all. And your fur family too!"

Every day, the family loved their sweet kitties. Unfortunately, the day came when Oreo got pretty sick. The Veterinarian had some grim news.

"Oreo has liver disease. His liver is not functioning well, and he may not live very long."

Everyone cried, but their Mom had a plan. She wanted to make sure that Oreo lived as long as he could, and she wanted to help make his last months as comfortable as possible. They tried different treatments for him, they served new foods to him, and they gave him lots of love and affection. They made sure that he had plenty of window time, so he could see those colorful birds.

However, after a while, it was time for Oreo to be put to sleep. But you know what happened? Their Mom and Dad had a plan for their family.

"Always know that it is ok to cry. Letting out our feelings is the best thing that we can do when we are sad. You can always talk to us about how you are doing. Remember to talk to your friends and other family members as well. And always know that you can talk to God too." Mom said.

As Dad got out the numerous photo albums, they all looked at the pictures of Oreo. They saw how everyone took turns holding him. "Remember all of the good times we had with him. Let's cherish all of the beautiful memories that we have of him."

Kalia picked up Bree, and held her in her arms like a baby. She said, "I will always be thankful for Bree. She is a treasure that I can hold in my arms. But I will always be thankful for Oreo as well, for he is the treasure that I can hold forever in my heart."

In loving memory of Oreo